Baby Sea Otter

Betty Tatham

illustrated by Joan Paley

Henry Holt and Company - New York

At the edge of the ocean, a baby sea otter is born. The mother lifts the wet pup onto her chest. With the claws of her forepaws she carefully grooms her baby.

The mother otter blows air bubbles into her pup's brown fur, where they will be trapped between the top layer of long hair and an underlayer of very thick fur. This helps keep the pup warm. The spring sun also warms the pup, who snuggles close. The mother coos and grunts as her baby nurses.

The mother grooms her own fur many times, day and night, to keep it waterproof. She also blows bubbles into her fur to make it warmer.

She spends most of her time lying on her back with her head, hind feet, and forepaws sticking out of the water. These parts of her body have little fur to keep them warm in the ocean, so she leaves them out of the cold water while she rests, grooms, or eats.

The mother otter is hungry. She needs to hunt for food at the bottom of the ocean. Her pup can float and swim but can't dive yet. To keep the baby from drifting away with the outgoing tide while she's gone, the mother places the pup on top of some kelp on the surface of the water. The kelp is anchored to rocks on the ocean floor. This keeps the pup in the kelp bed.

The mother has a furry pouch under each armpit where she carries things. She finds a clam and tucks it into the pouch under her left forearm. She also finds a crab, a sea urchin, and a useful flat stone.

Then she returns to the surface.

She puts her pup on her belly and uses her chest as a table. She sets the food on it, then takes the flat stone out of her pouch. She places the stone on her chest and bangs the clam against it until the shell breaks. She eats the tasty meat.

When she is finished, she rolls in the water to clean off. She grooms herself again. Then she wraps some slippery kelp strands around herself and her pup, and they rest for a while.

Suddenly the mother screams. A bald eagle is plunging toward her pup!

She grabs the pup and dives, paddling fast with her webbed feet and tail. The eagle's claws hit the water too late. The pup is safe!

The mother and her baby spend most of their time with other female otters and pups in a group called a raft. Their raft is in a kelp bed near the shore.

The pup sometimes plays with another pup. They swim together through the kelp bed or float on their backs. Sometimes they squeal.

The mother teaches her pup to dive and hunt for shellfish. They use their forepaws and long whiskers to feel for clams and crabs that are hidden in the sand. The pup can hold her breath underwater for only a short time, so every few minutes they swim up for air.

The pup is now big enough to swim around alone while the mother hunts for more food. An abalone clings to a big rock. The otter pounds the shellfish with a stone until it finally lets go.

The mother returns to the surface, but her pup is gone. *"Whee, whee!"* she whistles. She swims through their raft looking for her pup. No luck. Then she searches the jetty rocks, but the pup's not there, either.

Finally she hears her pup's voice. She speeds toward the sound. Her baby has been kidnapped by a male sea otter. He will not release the pup until the mother gives him the food she has in her pouch.

She lets go of her prey to grab the pup, whom the male releases so he can catch the food. The mother hisses and growls as she and the pup return to their raft.

At six months old, the pup has grown into a young sea otter. She no longer needs her mother's milk—she can find all her own food.

Now the young otter uses stones to crack open clams and to pry abalones loose. She breaks off the spines of a sea urchin before she eats it.

While most otters don't swim far from their raft, this one explores a little. Suddenly there is a great white shark racing toward her. The young otter swims as fast as she can, with her hind legs and tail going up and down, up and down.

The shark is getting closer.

Just then some dolphins jump out of the water near the shark. They could kill it by hitting it with their snouts, so the shark turns and swims away. With her heart pounding fast, the young otter safely reaches her raft in the kelp bed. From that day on, the otter is much more careful when she leaves the raft to search for food.

When the young otter is three years old she is ready to mate. Many males follow her. One is especially attentive. He greets her by swinging his head from side to side and nuzzling her fur. They stay together for about four days, mating, playing, and chasing each other.

About five months later, a pup is born. The young mother now lifts her own pup onto her chest.

With the claws of her forepaws she carefully grooms her baby. Then she coos and grunts to him, just as her own mother did when she was born.

Sea Otter Facts

Sea otters belong to the weasel family. They live in rafts that range in size from five to one thousand otters. Rafts are usually all male or all female, with pups staying with their mothers. Sea otters live along the shores of the Pacific Rim.

Males weigh about sixty pounds and are just over four feet long; females weigh around forty-five pounds and are just under four feet long. Sea otters can live as long as fifteen years. They have the thickest fur of any animal on earth. As many as one million hairs can be found in a patch the size of a quarter.

Sea otters were once hunted for their fur, and by the early 1900s there were fewer than two thousand left. Laws were passed in the United States and Canada to protect them, and now there are more than 150,000 sea otters, though in some places they are still endangered.

To the Monterey Bay Aquarium Sea Otter Research and Conservation Program, with special thanks to Michele Staedler. Also, deep appreciation to my wonderful editor, Reka Simonsen! —B. T.

To Judy Sue, who inspires us to make our art the best and most beautiful it can be, and to Philemon, whose wondrous words brighten our imagination. —J. P.

Henry Holt and Company, LLC, *Publishers since 1866*
115 West 18th Street, New York, New York 10011
www.henryholt.com

Henry Holt is a registered trademark of Henry Holt and Company, LLC
Text copyright © 2005 by Betty Tatham
Illustrations copyright © 2005 by Joan Paley
All rights reserved. Distributed in Canada by H. B. Fenn and Company Ltd.

Library of Congress Cataloging-in-Publication Data
Tatham, Betty. Baby sea otter / by Betty Tatham;
illustrated by Joan Paley.—1st ed.   p.   cm.
ISBN-13: 978-0-8050-7504-5
ISBN-10: 0-8050-7504-6
1. Sea otter—Juvenile literature. I. Paley, Joan, ill. II. Title.
QL737.C25T284 2005   599.769'5—dc22   2004023393
First Edition—2005 / Designed by Joan Paley and Donna Mark
Printed in China
10 9 8 7 6 5 4 3 2 1